Knit and Destroy

...gets handy!

D1337677

H46 674 843 8

Knit and Destroy… Gets Handy!
20 Projects That Put the 'Fun' in Functional
by Kandy Diamond.
© 2013 by Kandy Diamond.
All Rights Reserved. No part of this book may
be reproduced in any form without permission
in writing from the author/ publisher.
ISBN 978-0-9569059-2-5
Published by Cabin Creative, Manchester, UK.
(www.cabincreative.co.uk)
Printed by Bishops Printers.

Contents

Glasses Case; Page 38

CONTENTS

Pencil Scarf; Page 41

Introduction

Welcome to *Knit and Destroy Gets Handy…* I've enjoyed designing and making knitted creations for years now, with the help of my beloved knitting machines. More recently I've also ventured into the realms of hand knitting, and in this book you'll find a selection of my hand knit patterns so that you can enjoy recreating the items you'll see in here for yourselves. It seemed a shame to keep all of the fun to myself!

There are some simple patterns which are fun for everyone to make, including beginners, such as the Candy Cane Brooch and the Teacup Coasters. I've also included more advanced patterns like the 'I Heart Snow' scarf, and of course there's also plenty here for in-between knitters.

All patterns are clearly marked with a difficulty rating, to make it easy to decide which pattern is best for you. You'll also see me popping up throughout the book to give you handy knitting hints and tips. So go ahead, and I hope you'll enjoy knitting these woolly delights as much as I did.

Kandy

I first met Kandy Diamond, sparkling in sequined red hotpants, at the first UK *Bust* Christmas Craftacular in London, which I had organised with my friend Clare Chadburn.

Bust is a New York-based alternative women's magazine, which has long championed crafting, printing, DIY projects and how-to tips. Furthermore, in 2003, founding editor Debbie Stoller started a knitting group, and released a book of knitting patterns called *Stitch 'n' Bitch*. The media made much of this 'not your granny's' take on craft: knitting was cool, sewing was sexy, and cross-stitch, in the hands of Julie Jackson, was downright dirty.

Then, in 2005, *Bust* hosted its first Craftacular in Brooklyn; a craft fair that brought together designer-makers and which, in combining handmade goods with DJs, drinks and the magazine's reputation, helped to establish a new craft scene.

At that particular time, I was an intern at *Bust*. Back in London, I eventually – after co-editing a how-to book of 'alternative' craft projects called, *Making Stuff* – decided that a Craftacular would really go down a storm in the UK. ▷

One of the first applicants for a stall at this event was Knit and Destroy. From the cupcake cushions to the Casio watches and fox-shaped scarves, Kandy's quirky machine-knitted accessories chimed perfectly with the new pop-culture approach to craft.

'I want to make products that don't fit with the typical stereotype of knitting,' says Kandy, 'and in this way "destroy" people's preconceptions of the craft. Hence the name: Knit and Destroy.'

I want to make products that don't fit in with the typical stereotype of knitting.

Indeed, the arc of the Knit and Destroy label runs parallel with the development of this new 'craft movement'. As Kandy explains: 'In 2006, I started making scarves for a friend's existing label, which were sold at Manchester Student Market. At the time there wasn't the array of craft fairs that there are now. Then we found out about a Leeds craft fair called Pretty Crafty Things. And from there all sorts of craft fairs started popping up, such as Craft Candy at the Sheffield Millenium Gallery, and then the Craftacular.'

After the first London Craftacular we decided to move the event to a bigger venue, and now the event is over-subscribed several times over with a wealth of small businesses. But alongside those turning handmade goods into their livelihoods are those interested in craft as a hobby; an urge to do it

The Knit and Destroy stall at *Bust Craftacular*

yourself, which, unlike in previous generations, has not been borne out of necessity but rather a curiosity about the physicality of materials.

When I wrote my book *State of Craft*, of course I asked Kandy if she'd be willing to produce a hand-knit pattern for one of her Knit and Destroy designs. And just as Kandy's paintbrush scarf project helped to set the aesthetic tone then, this book is part and parcel of the current craft oeuvre: cool, a bit kitsch, slightly irreverent – and lots of fun.

Victoria Woodcock

Victoria Woodcock is a Maker, organiser of Bust's London Craftacular *and the writer behind the influential* State of Craft *blog (see www.stateofcraft.com).*

How to Use This Book

If you're reading this, that means you're about to delve into one of the knitting patterns I have designed for your enjoyment. I've put a few special components in this book to help make the knitting experience simple and enjoyable!

For instance, you will notice me popping up throughout the book with info, hints and tips to help you with the patterns...

... and each pattern will come with some essential information for you to read in the coloured, **Before You Start**, box. Read this carefully to avoid ending up with a gigantic green cat shaped throw, when what you were after was a chic cat scarf! ▷

In each
Before You Start
*box, you'll find the
following info:*

Videos

There are videos available for you to view online (made by me) which correspond to most of the techniques required in this book. You will read, for example: 'See video 1 for garter stitch'. To view this video go to the KandyKnits Youtube channel.

http://www.youtube.com/user/ KandyKnits/videos

Now select Video 1 – garter stitch. Then watch and follow the video as many times as you need to get the hang of that particular technique.

Instructionals

If you prefer printed instructions, knitting and sewing techniques along with diagrams can also be found on pages 71 to 78 of this book.

Difficulty Rating

Each pattern is marked with a number of balls of wool (see above). These signify the relative ease or difficulty of the pattern. So the more balls of wool there are, the trickier the pattern!

Finished Size

Read this so that you know what size to expect the item to come out.

Tension

This is super-important! You need to knit a tension square before you start the project, and then measure it to check it matches the given tension here. If it doesn't then simply change the needle size you're working on, change to smaller needle size if your knitting is too loose (if you have less stitches and rows per 10cm), or to larger needle size if your knitting is too tight (if you have more stitches and rows per 10cm).

Each pattern will also have a box entitled **You Will Need**. It is important that you read this and get all the tools and materials before you start your project. And please note: the yarn recommended is that which I used to make the products in the book. Feel free to use a different make or colour yarn if you like but if you do, be sure to knit a tension square! ❑

PATTERNS

LOVE TO CRAFT

Pin Cushion

Do you, like me, love making and mending but need somewhere to keep those pesky pins? What better way to show your love for stitching and keep organised, than by crafting this cute and handy heart-shaped pin cushion.

Before you start...

Difficulty Rating:

- Finished size of knitted pieces approx 12 cm by 10cm (smaller when sewn and stuffed).
- Tension, 20 stitches and 30 rows to 10cm over stocking stitch using 4mm needles.
- See video 5 for increase, video 6 for increase purl wise, video 8 for knit 2 together and video 9 for purl 2 together instructions.

You will need...

✓ Pair 4mm knitting needles.
✓ One ball King Cole Merino Blend DK wool in Scarlet.
✓ Stuffing.
✓ Tapestry needle.

Knitting

You need to make two identical heart shaped pieces, so follow these instructions through twice. Cast on 3 stitches.
Row 1: K1, inc1, k1. (4 sts)
Row 2: P1, inc1pw, p2. (5 sts)
Row 3: K1, inc1, k to the end of row.
Row 4: P1, inc1pw, p to the end of row.
Repeat rows 3 & 4 until you have 24 stitches, ending on a knit row.
Row 22: Purl all stitches.
Row 23: K1, K2tog twice, k7 and turn, place last 12 stitches from left needle on to a stitch holder. (You'll work on these stitches later).

Right Crest of the Heart

Working with 10 stitches on needles:
Row 1: P1, p2tog, p4, p2tog, p1. (8 sts)
Row 2: K1, k2tog twice, k3. (6 sts)
Row 3: P1, P2tog, p3. (5 sts)
Row 4: K1, K2tog twice. (3 sts)
Row 5: Sl 1, p2tog, psso. (1 st)
Cut yarn and pull through last st. Now slip 12 stitches from stitch holder back on needle and reattach yarn.

Left Crest of the Heart

Row 1: K7, k2tog twice, k1. (10sts)
Row 2: P1, p2tog, p4, p2tog, p1. (8 sts)
Row 3: K3, k2tog twice, k1. (6 sts)
Row 4: P3, p2tog, p1. (5 sts)
Row 5: K2tog twice, k1. (3 sts)
Row 6: Sl 1, p2tog, psso. (1 st)
Cut yarn and pull through last st.

Making up

Now you've knitted the front and the back of this pin cushion, block each piece. Place them together with the fronts facing out. Using mattress stitch, sew the hearts together, leaving a gap big enough to stuff. Stuff the pin cushion densely, sew up the gap and it's done! ❑

ALL TIED UP!

Menu

Bow Scarf

This cute bow scarf will add a touch of 'beau' to any outfit. Knitted in moss stitch this bow will stay pert and pretty!

Before you start...

Difficulty Rating:

● Finished size approx 11cm by 95cm
● Tension, 20 stitches and 36 rows to 10cm over moss stitch using 4mm needles.
● See instructions for moss stitch in 'main body of bow' section, or video 3.

You will need...

✓ Pair 4mm knitting needles.
✓ Two balls King Cole Merino Blend DK wool in Turquoise
✓ Tapestry needle.
✓ Tape measure.

Main Body of the Bow
Cast on 22 stitches.
Row 1: This pattern is worked in moss stitch, so from the first stitch: knit one, purl one, repeat across all 22 stitches.
Row 2: On the next row, from the first stitch: purl one, knit one, repeat across all 22 stitches.
Repeat Rows 1 and 2 to knit the body of the scarf in moss stitch, you need to knit until your piece measures 130cm.
Cast off.

Central Strip
Cast on 10 stitches.
Work in moss stitch for 60 rows. (See instructions for Main Body for moss stitch).
Cast off.

Making Up
Sew in any loose ends. Measure 20cm from the end and mark with a pin. Now measure 35 cm from this point and again, mark with a pin. Now fold the scarf bringing the 2 marked points together and pin the scarf together at this point (see diagram over page).
Now using your tapestry needle and the turquoise yarn, sew along this pinned line. Keeping the needle threaded, turn the work so that the scarf is facing you (see diagram). ▷

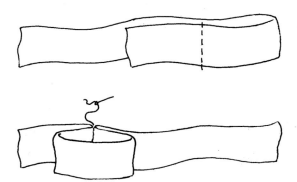

▲ **Creating the loop**

Now flatten the loop that you have just made; this will be the bow. You will now stitch down the centre of the bow using a running stitch so that it can be gathered. Pull the yarn to gather the centre of the bow. Wrap the yarn around the centre a few times, pull tight, tie off.

Take the central strip; place it over the centre you have just gathered. Stitch this piece at the top and bottom of the bow. Now join the ends behind the bow. This piece forms a loop that you will pass one end of the scarf through to secure it when you wear it! ❏

SWEET
TOOTH

For this cushion, you will knit two identical pieces; one will be the front and one the back of the cushion. Start with the cupcake case and work your way up...

Before you start...

Difficulty Rating:

- Finished size approx 38cm (at widest point) x 31cm.
- Tension: 20 stitches and 30 rows to 10cm over stocking stitch using 4mm needles.
- See video 5 for increase instructions, video 8 for knit two together instructions and video 10 for slipping stitches instructions.

You will need...

✓ Pair 4mm knitting needles.
✓ Four balls King Cole Merino Blend DK wool in Dusky Pink (*colour 1*).
✓ One ball King Cole Merino blend DK wool in Corn (*colour 2*).
✓ One ball King Cole Merino blend DK wool in Snow White (*colour 3*).
✓ Small amount of red yarn for pom-pom.
✓ Tapestry needle.
✓ Stuffing.

Cupcake Case
Using *Colour 1*, cast on 72 stitches.
Row 1: * K4, p2; rep from * to end.
Row 2: * K2, p4; rep from * to end.
Repeat rows 1 and 2 until you've worked 58 rows of this rib pattern.
Row 59: Purl all stitches.
Row 60: Knit all stitches.

The Cake
Change to *Colour 2*.
Row 61: Knit all stitches.
Row 62: Purl all stitches.
Row 63: Knit all stitches.
Row 64: Purl all stitches.
Row 65 (increase row): K1, inc1, k to last st, inc1, k1.
Row 66: Purl all stitches.
Repeat rows 61 – 66 once more. You will now have 76 stitches.

It's time to add the icing which we want to to sit in a pretty scalloped line on the top of this cupcake. ▷

The Icing

Change to *colour 3.*

Row 73: * Knit the first 5 stitches, slip the next 3 stitches onto the needle without working; repeat from * until you have 4 sts left on the needle, knit these 4 stitches.

Row 74: Purl the first 5 stitches, slip one stitch onto the needle without working, * purl 7 stitches, slip one stitch onto the needle without working; repeat from * until you have 6 sts left on the needle, purl these 6 stitches.

Row 75: Knit all stitches.

Row 76: Purl all stitches.

Row 77 (increase row): K1, inc1, k to last st, inc1, k1. (78 sts)

Row 78: Purl all stitches.

Row 79: Knit all stitches.

Repeat rows 78 and 79 twice more.

Row 84: Purl all stitches.

Row 85 (decrease row): K2tog, k to last 2 sts, k2tog.

Row 86: Purl all stitches.

Repeat rows 85 and 86 three more times. (70 sts).

Row 93: Knit all stitches.

Row 94: Purl all stitches. Cast off.

Make a second piece exactly the same, to use for the other side of the cushion.

Making Up

Sew in all loose yarn ends. Block both the pieces so they lie flat. Now taking your tapestry needle and corresponding coloured yarn, sew the pieces together using mattress stitch, leaving a gap of 10cm to stuff the cupcake.

Stuff the cupcake. Sew the gap closed. For the finishing touch, make a small pom-pom using the red yarn and a 7cm diameter cardboard circle (see **video 12** for instructions).

Now, using the tail of yarn left, stitch the pom-pom to the top of the cushion. ❑

ONE LUMP
OR TWO?

These coasters are simple, effective, and best of all, useful! Knitted in garter stitch they're perfect for beginners. As well as using the knit stitch you will also need to increase and decrease to complete them.

Before you start...

Difficulty Rating:

- Finished coaster measures approx 12 cm (at widest point, not including handle) by 11cm.
- Tension, 22 stitches and 44 rows to 10cm over garter stitch using 4mm needles.
- See video 1 for garter stitch, video 5 for increase and video 8 for knit two together instructions.

You will need...

✓ Pair 4mm knitting needles.
✓ One ball King Cole Merino Blend DK wool in Dusky Pink (*colour 1*).
✓ One ball King Cole Merino Blend DK wool in Turquoise (*colour 2*).
✓ Tapestry needle.

Knitting the Teacup
Using 4mm needles and *colour 1*, cast on 20 stitches.
Rows 1 - 3: Knit all stitches.
Row 4 (decrease row): K1, k2tog, k to last 3 sts, k2tog, k1. (18 sts)
Rows 5 - 7: Knit all stitches.
Row 8 (decrease row): K1, k2tog, k to last 3 sts, k2tog, k1. (16 sts).

Change to *colour 2*.
Rows 9 – 10: Knit all stitches.
Change back to *colour 1*, and cut off *colour 2*.
Rows 11 – 12: Knit all stitches.
Row 13 (increase row): K1, inc 1, k to last 2 sts, inc1, k1. (18 sts).
Rows 14 -19: Knit all stitches.
Row 20 (increase row): K1, inc1, k to last 2 sts, inc1, k1. (20 sts).

Now repeat rows 14 – 20 three more times (knitting 6 rows then increasing for one row), you will end up with 26 stitches.
Rows 42 – 48: Knit all stitches.

Change to *colour 2*.
Row 49: Knit all stitches.
Cast off.

Knitting the Handle
Using 4mm needles and *colour 1*, cast on 4 stitches.
Knit 36 rows in garter stitch.
Cast off.

Making Up
After sewing in any loose ends, simply stitch the handle to the side of the teacup. Now I think it's time for a celebratory cup of tea! ❑

KNITS AHOY!

Anchor Scarf

This nautical-themed scarf will bring out the sailor in you! Knitted in stocking stitch with a moss stitch border and embroidered detail for that extra special touch.

Before you start...

Difficulty Rating:

- Finished size approx 17cm x 175cm
- Tension, 20 stitches and 30 rows to 10cm over stocking stitch using 4mm needles
- See video 1 for garter stitch, video 2 for stocking stitch and video 11 for stranded knitting instructions.

You will need...

- ✓ Pair 4mm knitting needles.
- ✓ Three balls King Cole Merino Blend DK wool in Royal Blue (*colour 1*).
- ✓ One ball King Cole Merino Blend DK wool in Snow White (*colour 2*).
- ✓ Tapestry needle.

Knitting the Scarf

Using *colour 1*, cast on 35 stitches.

Row 1: Knit all stitches.
Row 2: * K1, p1; rep from * to last st, k1.
Row 3: * K1, p1; rep from * to last st, k1.
Repeat rows 2 and 3 once more.
Row 6: K1, p1, k1, p1, k27, p1, k1, p1, k1.
Row 7: K1, p1, k1, p1, p27, p1, k1, p1, k1.

You are now working stocking stitch with a moss stitch border of four stitches each side, you will continue working this stitch pattern whilst following Anchor Chart 1 across the centre 27 sts. Work the chart from row 1 at the bottom to the top, remember the chart width doesn't include the moss stitch border.

Anchor Chart 1 (overleaf)

When you have completed the anchor, continue working in stocking stitch with moss stitch border (rows 6 and 7 above) in royal blue (colour 1) until your scarf measures 160cm, ending with a purl row of stocking stitch.

Now for the second anchor, follow Anchor Chart 2 across the centre 27 sts, again working from row 1 at the bottom to the top, and continuing in stocking stitch with moss stitch border. Remember the chart width doesn't include the moss stitch border. ▷

Knit and Destroy... Gets Handy!

Chart 1

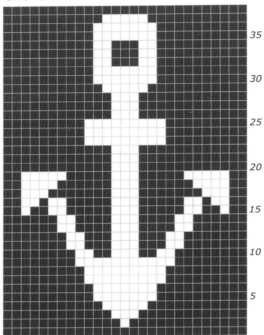

35
30
25
20
15
10
5

■ Colour 1
□ Colour 2

Anchor Chart 2

When you have completed the second anchor, knit 2 rows of the plain stocking stitch with moss stitch border followed by 4 rows of full moss stitch as written at beginning of scarf.
Cast off.

Making up

Sew in all loose yarn ends. Now to add that finishing touch, you will use a length of the white yarn and your tapestry needle to stitch on the anchor's rope. For this, use running stitch and follow the pattern shown on the close up photograph (below left).
Now you're ready to take to the high seas in style! ❏

Chart 2

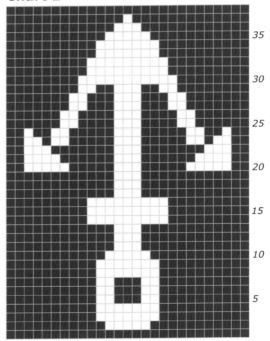

35
30
25
20
15
10
5

■ Colour 1
□ Colour 2

FLOWER
POWER

Rose Ring

Knitted in stocking stitch the natural curl of the knitting enhances the curved shape of the rose.

Before you start...

Difficulty Rating:

- Finished size made up, approx 4cm wide by 3cm high
- Tension, 20 stitches and 30 rows to 10cm over stocking stitch using 4mm needles.
- See video 2 for stocking stitch, video 5 for increase, and video 8 for knit two together instructions.

You will need...

✓ Pair 4mm knitting needles.
✓ One ball King Cole Merino Blend DK wool in Scarlet.
✓ Ring base.
✓ Hot melt glue gun.
✓ Tapestry Needle.

Knitting the Rose

Cast on 6 stitches.
Row 1: Knit all stitches.
Row 2: Purl all stitches.
Row 3 (increase row): Inc1, knit to end. (7sts)
Row 4: Purl all stitches.
Row 5: Knit all stitches.
Row 6: Purl all stitches.
Rows 7 -12: Repeat rows 5 and 6 three more times.
Row 13 (decrease row): K2tog, knit to end. (6sts)
Row 14: Purl all stitches.
Row 15: Knit all stitches.
Row 16: Purl all stitches.
Rows 17 – 20: Repeat rows 15 and 16 twice more.
Row 21 (decrease row): K2tog, knit to end. (5 sts)
Row 22: Purl all stitches.
Row 23: Knit all stitches.
Row 24: Purl all stitches.

Rows 25 – 28: Repeat rows 23 and 24 twice more.
Row 29 (decrease row): K2tog, knit to end. (4 sts)
Row 30: Purl all stitches.
Row 31: Knit all stitches.
Row 32: Purl all stitches.
Rows 33– 46: Repeat rows 31 and 32 seven more times.
Cast off and leave a 20cm tail of yarn.

Making Up

Your knitting will be a long thin strip, block it gently. To make it into a rose, curl the piece in a spiral shape with the thinner end in the centre. Stitch the layers of the spiral together at the bottom using the long tail of yarn, this stitching will be hidden when the rose is attached to the ring base. Now using your hot melt glue gun or other strong adhesive, stick the rose onto the ring base. ❑

STAY COOL!

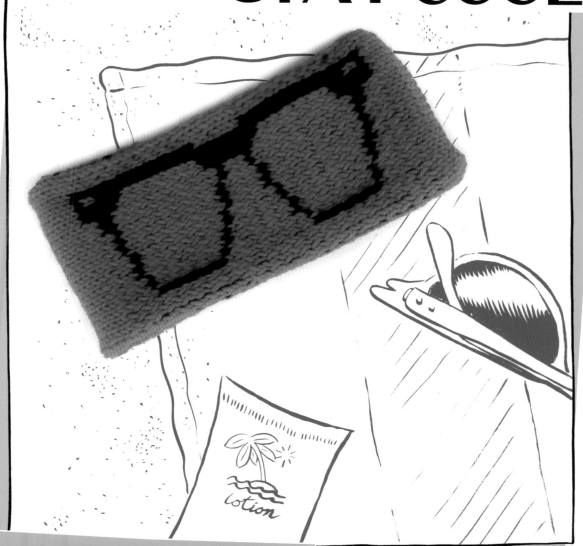

Sunglasses Case

Keep the sand off your sunglasses with this stylish case! When you're knitting the sunglasses pattern on the front, to ensure the surface stays smooth, don't pull the yarn too tight.

Before you start...

Difficulty Rating:

- Finished size when made up approx 9.5cm x 20cm (with flap closed)
- Tension, 23 stitches and 25 rows to 10cm over patterned stocking stitch using 4mm needles.
- See video 2 for stocking stitch and video 11 for stranded knitting instructions.

You will need...

- ✓ Pair 4mm knitting needles.
- ✓ One ball King Cole Merino Blend DK wool in Scarlet (*colour 1*).
- ✓ One ball King Cole Merino Blend DK wool in Black (*colour 2*).
- ✓ Tapestry needle.
- ✓ One black button.
- ✓ Sewing needle and black thread.

Knitting the Case
Using *colour 1*, cast on 44 stitches. Now working in stocking stitch (knit one row, purl one row) you will work through the chart, picking up *colour 2* on the 28th stitch of the first knitted row. You will then continue to work in two colours keeping the alternate yarn with you as you knit by stranding both colours across the back of the work by twisting them as you go. Work until you have finished row 49.

Sunglasses Chart (opposite)
Row 50: Using *colour 1*, cast off 22 sts (these will be the ones that will form the back of the case). Purl across the remaining 22 sts to make the flap. ▷

Chart

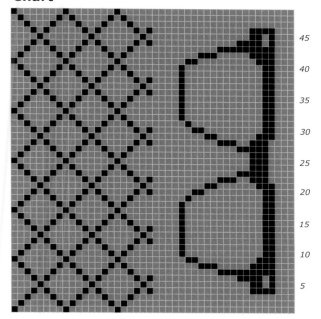

45
40
35
30
25
20
15
10
5

■ *Colour 1*
■ *Colour 2*

Making Up
Sew in all loose yarn ends. Sew the button onto the back of the glasses case. Now fold the case in half so the back of the knitting is facing you and stitch across the bottom and up the side of the case. ❏

Knitting the Flap
Row 1: Knit across all 17 stitches.
Row 2: Purl across all 17 stitches.
Rows 3-12: Repeat rows 1 and 2 five more times.
Row 13: Knit 10 stitches, cast off 2 stitches, knit 10 stitches.
Row 14: Purl 10 stitches, cast on 2 sts, purl 10 stitches.
Row 14: Knit all stitches.
Row 15: Purl all stitches.
Repeat rows 14 and 15 once more.
Cast off.

TOTALLY SWEET!

Cherry Scarf

This sweet cherry scarf will bring a taste of summer to even the coldest of winter days. keeping you warm and cosy and adding a splash of colour to any outfit!

Before you start...

Difficulty Rating:

- Finished size approx 18cm x 185cm.
- Tension, 20 stitches and 30 rows to 10cm over stocking stitch using 4mm needles.
- See video 2 for stocking stitch, video 3 for moss stitch and video 11 for stranded knitting instructions.

You will need...

- ✓ Pair 4mm knitting needles.
- ✓ Four balls King Cole Merino Blend DK wool in Black (colour 1).
- ✓ One ball King Cole Merino Blend DK wool in Scarlet (colour 2).
- ✓ One ball King Cole Merino Blend DK wool in Fern (colour 3)
- ✓ Tapestry needle.

Knitting the Scarf
Using *colour 1*, cast on 37 stitches.
Row 1: Knit all stitches.
Row 2: * K1, p1; rep from * to last st, k1.
Row 3: * K1, p1; rep from * to last st, k1.
Repeat rows 2 and 3 once more.
Row 6: K1, p1, k1, p1, k29, p1, k1, p1, k1.
Row 7: K1, p1, k1, p1, p29 , p1, k1, p1, k1.

You are now working in stocking stitch with a moss stitch border of 4 stitches each side, you will continue working this stitch pattern whilst following Cherry Chart 1 across the centre 29 sts. Work the chart from row 1 at the bottom to the top, remember the chart width doesn't include the moss stitch border.

Cherry Chart 1 (overleaf)
When you have completed the cherry, continue working in stocking stitch with moss stitch border (rows 6 and 7 above) in black *(colour 1)* until your scarf measures 170cm, ending with a purl row of stocking stitch.

Now for the second cherry, follow Cherry Chart 2 (overleaf) across the centre 29 sts, again working from row 1 at the bottom to top, and continuing in stocking stitch with moss stitch border. Remember the chart width doesn't include the moss stitch border. ▷

Knit and Destroy... Gets Handy!

Chart 1

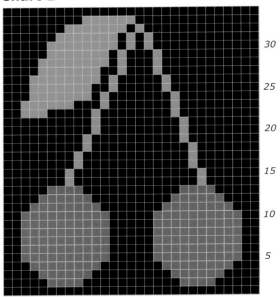

30
25
20
15
10
5

■ Colour 1
■ Colour 2
■ Colour 3

Cherry Chart 2 (Below)
When you have completed the second cherry, knit 2 rows of the plain stocking stitch with moss stitch border followed by 4 rows of full moss stitch as written at the beginning of the scarf.
Cast off and enjoy!

If you want to add some extra juice to your cherry scarf, you can make 4 half pompoms and stitch them over the knitted cherries. ❑

Chart 2

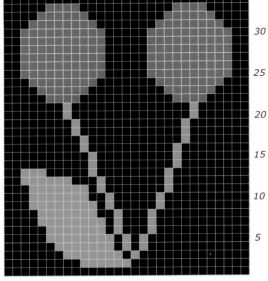

30
25
20
15
10
5

■ Colour 1
■ Colour 2
■ Colour 3

A STITCH IN TIME

Knitted Watch

It can be your favourite time of day all day long with this knitted wristwatch — and the battery never runs out! This watch is knitted with a rib strap and a stocking stitch face.

Before you start...

Difficulty Rating:

- Finished size approx 5cm (at the widest point) x 24cm.
- Tension, 30 stitches and 28 rows to 10cm over k1, p1 rib using 4mm needles.
- See video 4 for Knit one, Purl one rib, video 2 for stocking stitch, and video 9 for Purl two together.

You will need...

✓ Pair 4mm knitting needles.
✓ One ball King Cole Merino Blend DK wool in Black (colour 1).
✓ Small amount of King Cole Merino Blend DK wool in Pale Grey (colour 2).
✓ One black button.
✓ Sewing needle and black thread.
✓ Tapestry needle.

Knitting

Using *colour 1*, cast on 7 stitches.
Row 1: (K1, p1) 3 times, k1.
Row 2: (P1, k1) 3 times, p1.
Work 20 more rows in rib by repeating rows 1 and 2 ten times.
Row 23: Knit all stitches.
Change to *colour 2*.
Row 24: Purl all stitches
Change back to *colour 1*.
Row 25 (increase row): K1, inc1, k to last st, inc1, k1.(9 sts)
Row 26: purl all stitches
Row 27 (increase row): K1, inc1, k to last st, inc1, k1. (11 sts)
Rows 28 – 31: Now continuing to work in stocking stitch, starting with a purl row, work across 11 sts of this chart.

Watch Chart

Working in *colour 1*.
Row 32 (decrease row): P2tog, p to last 2 sts, p2tog. (9 sts)
Row 33: Knit all stitches.
Row 34 (decrease row): P2tog, p to last 2 sts, p2tog. (7 sts)
Row 35: Knit all stitches
Change to *colour 2*.
Row 36: Purl all stitches.
Change to *colour 1*, you are now going to work the second watch strap in k1, p1 rib.
Row 37 -54: Rib all stitches by repeating rows 1 and 2. ▷

Row 55: K1, p1, k1, p2tog, p1, k1.

Row 55: K1, p1, k1, bring the yarn forward between the needles and then take it over the needle, k2tog, p1, k1.

Rows 57 – 60: Rib all stitches. Cast off.

Making Up

Using your tapestry needle and yarn in *colour 1*, stitch on whatever time of day you would like your watch to read.

Now thread your needle with *colour 2* and make three French knots for the buttons on your watch (see photograph, right, for placement).

Now find the perfect place for your button by trying the watch on your wrist. Mark where the button needs to go, take the watch off and sew on the button. ❑

Chart

▉   *Colour 1*

☐   *Colour 2*

TRULY
SPEC-TACULAR!

Glasses Case

They say that boys don't make passes at girls who wear glasses. I say that's nonsense! Especially when they're kept in such a fancy case.

Before you start...

Difficulty Rating:

- Finished size when made up approx 7.5 cm by 20cm (with flap closed)
- Tension, 23 stitches and 25 rows to 10cm over patterned stocking stitch using 4mm needles
- See video 2 for stocking stitch and video 11 for stranded knitting instructions.

You will need...

✓ Pair 4mm knitting needles.
✓ One ball King Cole Merino Blend DK wool in Petrol Blue (*colour 1*).
✓ One ball King Cole Merino Blend DK wool in Dusky Pink (*colour 2*).
✓ Tapestry needle.
✓ Sew-on diamantes.
✓ Sewing needle and thread.
✓ Pink button.

Knitting the Case

Using *colour 1*, cast on 34 stitches Now working in stocking stitch (knit one row, purl one row) you will work through the chart, picking up *colour 2* on the 19th stitch of the first knitted row.

You will then continue to work in two colours keeping the alternate yarn with you as you knit by stranding both colours across the back of the work by twisting them as you go. Work until you have finished row 49.

Glasses Chart

Row 50: Using *colour 1*, cast off 17 sts (these will be the ones that will form the back of the case), purl across the remaining 17 sts to make the flap.

Knitting the Flap

Row 1: Knit across all 17 stitches.
Row 2: Purl across all 17 stitches.
Rows 3-12: Repeat rows 1 and 2 five more times.
Row 13: Knit 8 stitches, cast off 2 stitches, knit 7 stitches. ▷

Chart

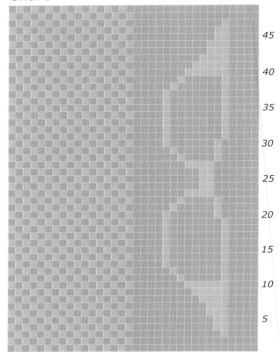

45
40
35
30
25
20
15
10
5

■ Colour 1
■ Colour 2

Row 14: Purl 8 stitches, cast on 2 sts, purl 6 stitches.
Row 15: Knit all stitches.
Row 16: Purl all stitches.
Repeat rows 15 and 16 once more.
Cast off.

Making Up
Sew in all loose yarn ends. Sew on the diamantes in place onto the glasses, and the button on the back. Fold the case in half so the back of the knitting is facing you and stitch across the bottom and up the side of the case. Now turn it the right way out and pop your glasses in it! ❑

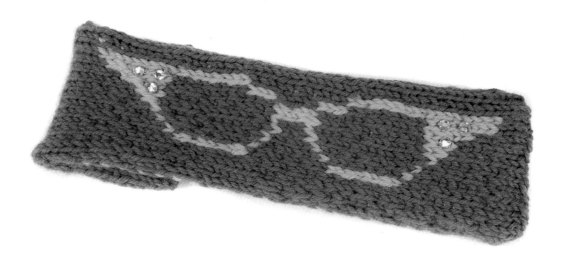

Pencil Scarf

This pencil scarf will be knitted in stocking stitch. You will start with the eraser and end with the point!

Difficulty Rating:

- Finished size approx 12.5cm by 175cm.
- Tension, 20 stitches and 30 rows to 10cm over stocking stitch using 4mm needles.
- See video 2 for stocking stitch and video 8 for knit two together instructions.

You will need...

- ✓ Pair 4mm knitting needles.
- ✓ One ball King Cole Merino Blend DK wool in Dusky Pink (*colour 1*).
- ✓ One ball King Cole Merino Blend DK wool in Pale Grey (*colour 2*).
- ✓ Three balls King Cole Merino Blend DK wool in Black (*colour 3*).
- ✓ Three balls King Cole Merino blend DK wool in Scarlet (*colour 4*).
- ✓ One ball King Cole Merino blend DK wool in Beige (*colour 5*).
- ✓ Tapestry needle.

Knitting

Using *colour 1*, cast on 21 stitches.
Row 1: Knit all stitches.
Row 2: Purl all stitches.
Row 3 (increase row): K1, inc1, k to last 2 sts, inc1, k1. (23 sts)
Row 4: Purl all stitches.
Row 5 (increase row): K1, inc1, k to last 2 sts, inc1, k1. (25 sts)
Row 6: Purl all stitches
Rows 7–16: Work stocking stitch by repeating rows 1 and 2.

Change to *colour 3*.
You are moving on to the metal part now.
Rows 17 to 32: Still working in stocking stitch, work in stripe pattern of one row *colour 3* (black), four rows *colour 2* (pale grey), one row *colour 3*, four rows *colour 2*, one row *colour 3*, four rows *colour 2*, one row *colour 3*.

Now you have knitted the 'eraser' and the 'metal piece' we are going to move on to the main body of the pencil. For this part you will be working in two colours: red and black. Before you start, wind three balls of red and two of black to work with. You can wind these onto yarn holders or put them in small bags to help keep them separate as you work. Now, knitting stocking stitch, follow the chart below:

Pencil Chart (opposite page)
Remember, when you are swapping colours, you need to twist the yarns together to keep ▷

your work joined and avoid any gaps between these vertical columns of colour.

Repeat the two rows from the chart until the scarf measures 160cm, ending on a knit row.

Getting to the Point...
Change to beige *(colour 5)*.
Row 1: Purl all stitches.
Row 2: Knit all stitches.
Row 3: Purl all stitches.
Row 4 (decrease row): K2tog, k to last 2 sts, k2tog.
Repeat rows 1 to 4 six more times. (11sts) (28 rows have been worked)
Row 29: Purl all stitches.

Change to black *(colour 3)*.
Row 30: Knit all stitches.
Row 31: Purl all stitches.
Row 32 (decrease row): K2tog, k to last 2 sts, k2tog. (9 sts)
Row 33: Purl all stitches.
Row 34: Knit all stitches.
Row 35: Purl all stitches.
Row 36 (decrease row): K2tog, k to last 2 sts, k2tog. (7 sts)

Chart

■ *Colour 4*
■ *Colour 3*

Row 37: Purl all stitches.
Row 38 (decrease row): K2tog, k3, k2tog. (5 sts)
Row 39: Purl all stitches.
Row 40 (decrease row): K2tog, k1, k2tog.
Cast off.

Making up
Simply sew in any loose ends and block the scarf. This scarf will roll up on itself, so as you block each section, fold the scarf up, keeping it flat. Then place on top of a radiator to dry through. When it's dry, take it off the radiator, place it round your neck and look sharp for the winter. ❏

MR. BOOKWORM

This cute little bookworm is perfect for any book-lover. He'll help you keep your place and won't eat the pages. You could even use him to mark your page in this very book!

Before you start...

Difficulty Rating:

- Finished size approx 5cm (at widest point) by 25cm.
- Tension, 20 stitches and 30 rows to 10cm over stocking stitch using 4mm needles.
- See video 2 for stocking stitch, video 5 for increase and video 8 for knit two together.

You will need...

- ✓ Pair 4mm knitting needles.
- ✓ One ball King Cole Merino Blend DK yarn in Forest.
- ✓ Small amount of black yarn.
- ✓ Small amount of blue yarn.
- ✓ Tapestry needle.

Knitting
Mr Bookworm will be knitted in stocking stitch.

To make the body:
Cast on 7 sts.
Row 1: Knit all stitches.
Row 2: Purl all stitches.
Now repeat rows 1 and 2 until your piece measures 20cm.

For the head:
Row 1: K1, inc1, k3, inc1, k1.
Row 2: Purl all 9 stitches.
Row 3: K1, inc1, k5, inc1, k1.
Row 4: Purl all 11 stitches.
Row 5: Knit all stitches.
Row 6: Purl all stitches.
Rows 7–10: Repeat rows 5 and 6 twice.

Now to decrease the head:
Row 11: K1, k2tog, k5, k2tog, k1.
Row 12: Purl all 9 stitches.
Row 13: K1, k2tog, k3, k2tog, k1.
Row 14: Purl all 7 stitches.
Cast off.

Making up
Sew in any loose ends and block the bookworm until he lies flat. Now using the black yarn and referring to the photograph, stitch on a smile and a pair of glasses. Then using the blue, make two French knots for the bookworm's eyes. ❏

PURRRRFECT!

Smoky the Cat Cushion

You can tell by the satisfied smile on his face that Smoky is a very contented cat! Big, soft and cosy, he's the perfect sofa companion for those chilly winter evenings.

Before you start...

Difficulty Rating:

- Finished size: approx 32cm (at widest point) x 28cm.
- Tension, 20 stitches and 30 rows to 10cm over stocking stitch using 4mm needles.
- See video 1 for garter stitch, video 5 for increase, video 8 for knit two together, video 9 for purl two together, and video 11 for stranded knitting instructions.

You will need...

✓ Pair 4mm knitting needles.
✓ Three balls King Cole Merino blend DK wool in Pale Grey (*colour 1*).
✓ One ball King Cole Merino Blend DK wool in Black (*colour 2*).
✓ One ball King Cole Merino blend DK wool in Dusky Pink (*colour 3*).
✓ Stuffing.
✓ Tapestry needle.
✓ Two stitch holders.

To make this cushion, you will be knitting a front and a back piece. These will both be knitted in stocking stitch, the front will have the cat's face on, and the back will be plain. Both pieces are shaped; follow the shape shown on the chart, using the knitting twice into one stitch increase method.

Knitting
Using *colour 1*, cast on 43 sts. Follow the patterning and shaping on the chart, working in stocking stitch as follows:
Row 1: Knit all stitches.
Row 2: Purl all stitches.
Row 3 (increase row): Inc1, k to last st, inc1.
Row 4: Purl all stitches.
Continue to work from the chart until you have finished row 70.

Smoky Chart
For detail on the face and ears use the stranding knitting technique; twisting the old colour over the new colour to be used to prevent a hole appearing in the work.
To knit the ears (same for the back and the front):
Pattern 12 stitches (start of the right ear), place the next 53 stitches on to a stitch holder. ▷

CAT CUSHION

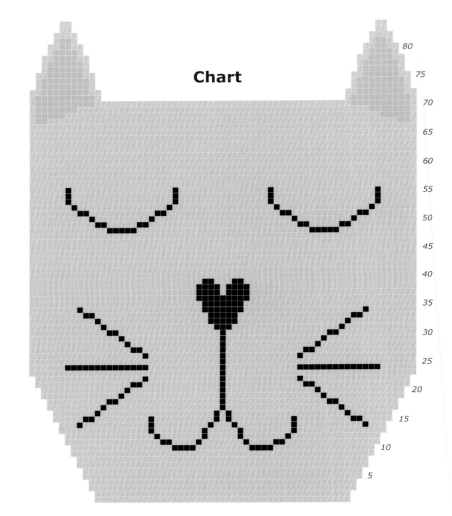

Chart

Colour 1
Colour 2
Colour 3

Knitting the right ear
Working on the 12 stitches on the needle, follow the chart, decreasing stitches where shown by working k2tog at each end of knit rows and p2tog at each end of purl rows. Work until you have finished row 84, you will have 2 stitches left.
K2tog, cut yarn and pull through the last stitch.

The middle section
Slip 41 Stitches from the large stitch marker onto the main needles and cast all the stitches off. Tie off at the last stitch.

Knitting the left ear
Slip stitches from stitch holder back on to the needle, reattach *colour 1* and cast off 41 stitches then knit to the end.
The remaining 12 sts are the start of the left ear. Work in the same way as the right ear.

Back
Follow the chart working the shaping the same as the front, using *colour 1* only.

Making up
Sew in all loose yarn ends. Place the front and back together, with the right sides facing out, pin together and stitch together using mattress stitch and the pale grey yarn, leaving a gap big enough to stuff it. Now stuff well then sew up the gap you left using the same technique. ❏

MAKE AN
IMPRESSION

Paintbrush Tie

This paintbrush tie is perfect for when you need to dress smart but still want to express your inner artist! I've used petrol blue for the tip of the brush, but you can pick your favourite colour instead.

Before you start...

Difficulty Rating:

- Finished size approx 5cm (at widest point) by 132cm.
- Tension, 30 stitches and 28 rows to 10cm over k1, p1 rib using 4mm needles.
- See video 4 for Knit one, Purl one rib, video 9 for Purl two together, video 8 for knit two together, and video 7 for rib increase instructions.

You will need...

✓ Pair 4mm knitting needles.
✓ One ball King Cole Merino Blend DK wool in Black (colour 1).
✓ One ball King Cole Merino Blend DK wool in Pale Grey (*colour 2*).
✓ One ball King Cole Merino Blend DK wool in Beige (*colour 3*).
✓ One ball King Cole Merino blend DK wool in Petrol Blue (*colour 4*).
✓ Tapestry needle.

Knitting the Paintbrush
Using *colour 1*, cast on 9 stitches. The paintbrush is worked in knit 1, purl 1 rib:
Row 1: K1, * p1, k1; repeat from * to end.
Row 2: P1, * k1, p1; repeat from * to end.
Repeat rows 1 and 2 until the piece measures 90cm. ▷

You are now going to start increasing to shape the paintbrush.
Row 1 (increase row): (P1, k1) into first st, rib to last st, (k1, p1) into last st. (11 sts)
Rows 2 – 15: Rib all stitches.
Row 16 (increase row): (P1, k1) into first st, rib to last st, (k1, p1) into last st. (13 sts)
Rows 17 – 30: Rib all stitches.
Row 31 (increase row): (P1, k1) into first st, rib to last st, (k1, p1) into last st. (15 sts)
Rows 32 – 51: Rib all stitches. ▷

Change to *colour 2*.
Rows 52- 54: Rib all stitches.

Change to *colour 1*.
Row 55: Rib all stitches.

Change to *colour 2*.
Rows 56-57: Rib all stitches.
Row 58 (decrease row): P2tog, rib to last 2 sts, p2tog. (13 sts

Change to *colour 1*.
Row 59: Rib all stitches.

Change to *colour 2*.
Rows 60-63: Rib all stitches.
Row 64 (decrease row): K2tog, rib to last 2 sts, k2tog. (11 sts)
Rows 65 – 69: Rib all stitches.
Row 70 (decrease row): P2tog, rib to last 2 sts, p2tog. (9 sts)
Rows 71–74: Rib all stitches.
Row 75 (decrease row): P2tog, rib to last 2 sts, p2tog. (7 sts).

Change to *colour 1*.
Row 76: Rib all stitches.

Now to knit the bristles and the paint:
Change to *colour 3*.
Rows 77-78: Rib all stitches.
Row 79 (increase row): (K1, p1) into first stitch, rib to last st, (p1, k1) into last stitch. (9 sts) ▷

Rows 80-81: Rib all stitches.
Row 82 (increase row): (K1, p1) into first stitch, rib to last st, (p1, k1) into last stitch. (11 sts)
Rows 83-84: Rib all stitches
Row 85 (increase row): (K1, p1) into first stitch, rib to last st, (p1, k1) into last stitch. (13 sts)
Rows 86-87: Rib all stitches

Change to *colour 4*.
Rows 88-89: Rib all stitches.
Row 90 (decrease row): K2tog, rib to last 2 sts, k2tog. (11 sts)
Row 91: Rib all stitches.
Row 92 (decrease row): P2tog, rib to last 2 sts, p2tog. (9 sts)
Row 93: Rib all stitches.
Row 94 (decrease row): K2tog, rib to last 2 sts, k2tog. (7 sts)
Row 95: Rib all stitches.
Row 96 (decrease row): P2tog, rib to last 2 sts, p2tog. (5 sts)
Row 97 (decrease row): P2tog, k1, p2tog.
Cast off.

Sew in all the loose ends and wear your paintbrush with pride!

FELINE WARM!

Cat Scarf

This scarf is the perfect winter accessory for any cat lover. Knitted in rib, this scarf is thick and super comfy.

Before you start...

Difficulty Rating:

- Finished size approx 11cm x 123cm (including tail).
- Tension, 30 stitches and 28 rows to 10cm over k1, p1 rib using 4mm needles.
- See video 4 for Knit one, Purl one rib, video 9 for Purl two together, video 8 for knit two together, and video 7 for rib increase instructions.

You will need...

- ✓ Pair 4mm knitting needles.
- ✓ Two balls King Cole Merino Blend DK yarn in Graphite.
- ✓ Small amount of grey and pink yarns for face detail.
- ✓ Tapestry needle.
- ✓ Stitch holder.

For this scarf, you will start at the bottom with the feet and work your way up to the head. When increasing, with instruction (k1, p1) into stitch, make sure that you work into the front, then the back of the stitch.

Foot
Cast on 6 stitches.
Row 1: K1, p1, repeat across all 6 stitches.
Row 2 (increase row): (P1, k1) into first st * p1, k1; rep from * to last stitch, (p1, k1) into last stitch.
You will now have 8 stitches.
Rows 3 – 10: P1, k1, repeat to end.
Slip these foot stitches onto your stitch holder.

Tail
Cast on 6 stitches
Row 1: (K1, p1), repeat to end.

Row 2 (increase row): (P1, k1) into first st * p1 k1; rep from * to last stitch, (p1, k1) into last stitch.
You will now have 8 stitches.
Rows 3 – 36: (P1, k1), repeat to the end.

Slip these tail stitches onto the stitch holder along with the foot you've already knitted.
Now following the previous foot instructions, knit another foot. When you've completed this foot, link the feet and tail together as follows: Rib across foot, cast on 4 sts, slip tail stitches back onto ▷

the needle and rib across them, cast on 4 sts, slip feet stitches back onto needle and rib across them (32 sts).
Phew, that was tricky!
Now for a long stretch of straight knitting.

The Body
Row 1: (P1, k1), repeat across all 32 stitches on needle.
Continue working in p1, k1 rib until the body measures 100cm.

Neck and Head
Now to shape the cat's neck and head.
Row 1 (decrease row): K2tog *p1, k1; rep from * to last 2 sts, p2tog. (30 sts)

Row 2: (K1, p1), repeat to end.
Row3 (decrease row): P2tog, *k1, p1; rep from * to last 2 sts, k2tog. (28 sts)
Rows 4 & 5: (P1, k1), repeat to end.
Row 6 (increase row): (K1, p1) into first st *k1, p1, rep from * to last st, (k1, p1) into last st. (30 sts)
Row 7: (K1, p1), repeat to end.
Row 8 (increase row): (P1, k1) into first st *p1, k1, rep from * to last st, (p1, k1) into last st. (32 sts)
Row 9: (P1, k1), repeat to end.
Row 10 (increase row): (K1, p1) into first st *k1, p1, rep from * to last st, (k1, p1) into last st. (34 sts)
Rows 11 – 24: (K1, p1), repeat to end.
Row 25 (decrease row): P2tog, * k1, p1; rep from * to last 2 sts, k2tog.
Row 26 (decrease row): K2tog * p1, k1; rep from * to last 2 sts, p2tog.

Repeat rows 25 and 26 once more. (26 sts)
Cast off.

Ears
Cast on 12 stitches.
Row 1: (K1, p1), repeat to end.
Row 2 (decrease row): P2tog *k1, p1; rep from * to last 2 sts, k2tog.
Row 3 (decrease row): K2tog *p1, k1; rep from * to last 2 sts, p2tog.
Row 4: (K1, p1), repeat to end.
Row 5 (decrease row): P2tog, (k1, p1) twice, k2tog.
Row 6 (decrease row): K2tog, p1, k1, p2tog.
Row 7: (K1, p1), repeat to end.
Row 8 (decrease row): P2tog, k2tog.
Cast off.

Making Up
Sew in all loose yarn ends. Now using your tapestry needle and the charcoal wool, stitch the ears in position as shown on close-up photograph. For the finishing touch, stitch the cat's smiley face on using running stitch! ❏

LITTLE BEAU PEEP

Bow Brooch

This cute little bow is a very simple pattern; knitted in garter stitch it is perfect for the beginner! This colourful bow can be added to your cardigan, hat, coat or bag to brighten your day.

Before you start...

Difficulty Rating

- Finished size, when made up, approx 9cm by 6cm.
- Tension, 22 stitches and 44 rows to 10cm over garter stitch (knitting all stitches every row) using 4mm needles.
- See video 1 for garter stitch instructions.

You will need...

✓ Pair 4mm knitting needles.
✓ One ball King Cole Merino Blend DK wool in Turquoise (*colour 1*).
✓ One ball King Cole Merino Blend DK wool in Dusky Pink (*colour 2*).
✓ Tapestry needle.
✓ Brooch back.
✓ Sewing needle and thread.

Knitting

For the main body:
Using *colour 1*, cast on 14 stitches.
Knit 40 rows in garter stitch (knitting all stitches every row).
Cast off.

For the central strip:
Using *colour 2,* cast on 4 stitches.
Knit 33 rows in garter stitch (knitting all stitches every row).
Cast off.

Making up:
Sew in any loose ends on the main piece. Now, you will fix the central strip round the middle of the bow. First pinch the main piece of the bow in the centre. Next place the strip here and using your tapestry needle and yarn in *colour 2*, stitch the ends of the central strip together behind the bow. Now using your sewing needle and thread, stitch your brooch back to the bow! ❑

FUR FREE!

Fox Scarf

To knit this friendly fox you will start at the bottom and work your way up to the head.

Before you start...

Difficulty Rating:

● Finished size approx 12.5cm (at widest point) by 95cm.
● Tension, 30 stitches and 28 rows to 10cm over k1, p1 rib using 4mm needles.
● See video 4 for Knit 1, Purl one rib, video 9 for Purl two together, video 8 for knit two together, and video 7 for rib increase instructions.

You will need...

✓ Pair 4mm knitting needles.
✓ Stitch holder.
✓ Two balls King Cole Merino Blend DK wool in Copper (*colour 1*).
✓ One ball King Cole Merino Blend DK wool in Snow White (*colour 2*).
✓ Small amount of black yarn to stitch eyes on.
✓ Black button.
✓ Sewing needle and black thread.
✓ 10cm of 3mm wide flat black elastic.

Foot
Using *colour 1*, cast on 6 stitches.
Row 1: (K1, p1) repeat to end
Row 2 (increase row): (P1, k1) into first st, * p1 k1; rep from * to last stitch, (p1, k1) into last st. You will now have 8 stitches.
Rows 3 – 10: (P1, k1) repeat to end.
Slip these foot stitches onto your stitch holder.

Tail
Using *colour 2*, cast on 8 stitches.
Rows 1 - 2: (K1, p1) repeat to end.
Row 3 (increase row): (P1, k1) into first st, * p1, k1; rep from * to last st, (p1, k1) into last st.
Row 4: (P1, k1) repeat to end.
Row 5 (increase row): (K1, p1) into first st, * k1, p1; rep from * to last st, (k1, p1) into last st.
Row 6: (K1, p1) repeat to end
Rows 7 – 18: Repeat rows 3-6

three more times, you will have 24 stitches.

Change to *colour 1*.
Work 8 rows in k1, p1 rib.
Row 25 (decrease row): P2tog, * k1, p1; rep from * to last 2 sts, k2tog.
Rows 26 -27: (P1, k1) repeat to end.
Row 28 (decrease row): K2tog, *p1, k1; rep from * to last 2 sts, p2tog.
Rows 29 - 30: (K1, p1) repeat to end.
Repeat rows 25 – 30 three more times, you will have 8 stitches. Slip this tail onto the stitch holder along with the foot you've already knitted.

Now following the previous instructions, knit another foot. When you have completed this ▷

foot, do not break the yarn, and using this yarn, keeping the pattern correct, rib across 8 sts of the foot, cast on 3 sts, rib across 8 sts of the top of the tail, cast on 3sts then rib across 8 sts of the second foot. You'll now have 30sts on your needle; these 30 stitches make the foundation of the body. Phew, that was tricky! Now for a long stretch of straight knitting.

The Body
Row 1: (P1, k1) repeat across all 30 stitches on needle.
Continue working in p1, k1 rib until the body (not including the feet and tail) measures 60cm.

The Head
Row 1 (increase row): (K1, p1) into first st, * k1, p1; rep from * to last st, (k1, p1) into last st.
Rows 2 – 3: (K1, p1) repeat to end.
Row 4 (increase row): (P1, k1) into first st, * p1, k1; rep from * to last st, (p1, k1) into last st.
Rows 5 – 7: (P1, k1) repeat to end
Row 8 (increase row): (K1, p1) into first st, * k1, p1; rep from * to last st, (k1, p1) into last st.
Rows 9 – 10: (K1, p1) to end.
Row 11 (increase row): (P1, k1) into first st, * p1, k1; rep from * to last st, (p1, k1) into last st.
Row 12: (P1, k1) repeat to end.
You will now have 38 stitches on your needle.
Row 13: (P1, k1) repeat to end.
Row 14 (decrease row): K2tog, * p1, k1; rep from * to last 2 sts, p2tog.
Row 15 (decrease row): P2tog, * k1, p1; rep from * to last 2 sts, k2tog.
Repeat rows 14 and 15 until you have 6 stitches.
Cast off.

You will be positioning the ears symmetrically (see photo, above right). These will be knitted straight onto the fox's head by picking up stitches.

Ears
Turn head so the nose is towards you and the right side of the knitting is facing you.
Pick up the first two loops of plain stitch on the outside edge at your chosen position, then the next two loops of plain stitch on the same line, move one line up (away from nose), pick up a further four loops in the same way, move one line up, pick up a further four loops, you should have picked up twelve loops in total.

Row 1: (K1, p1) repeat across twelve picked up loops.
Row 2: (K1, p1) repeat to end.
Row 3 (decrease row): P2tog, * k1, p1; rep from * to last 2 sts, k2tog.
Row 4: (P1, k1) repeat to end.
Row 5 (decrease row): K2tog, * p1, k1; rep from * to last 2 sts, p2tog.

Row 6: (K1, p1) repeat to end.
Repeat rows 3 – 6 once more, you should have 4 stitches on the needle then repeat rows 3 and 4 once to take it down to 2 stitches. Cast off.

Repeat this process but on the other edge of the fox's head.

Bottom Jaw
Cast on 38 stitches in *colour 1*. Now follow the instructions for the head, from row 13 onwards to create the same triangular shaped piece as the head.

Making up
Line up the bottom jaw on the back of the head; stitch this on passing the yarn through the back of the stitches only so the stitches don't show on the front of the scarf.
   Now, stitch the button nose on to the face, and the black elastic in a loop on to the bottom jaw. The last finishing touch is to stitch on the eyes with the black yarn. ❑

SWEET
ON YOU!

Candy Cane Brooch

Quick and easy, this candy cane brooch is knitted in stocking stitch and is perfect for beginners. See your straight piece of striped knitting become transformed into a wearable candy cane with the addition of a pipe cleaner and a brooch back.

Before you start...

Difficulty Rating:

- Finished size of brooch approx 4cm by 7.5cm.
- Tension, 20 stitches and 30 rows to 10cm over stocking stitch using 4mm needles.
- See video 2 for stocking stitch instruction.

You will need...

- ✓ Pair 4mm knitting needles.
- ✓ One ball King Cole Merino Blend DK wool in Snow White (*colour 1*).
- ✓ One ball King Cole Merino Blend DK wool in Scarlet (*colour 2*).
- ✓ White pipe cleaner.
- ✓ Brooch back.
- ✓ Tapestry needle.
- ✓ Sewing needle and thread.

Knitting

Using *colour 1*, cast on 6 stitches.
Row 1: Knit all stitches.
Row 2: Purl all stitches.
Change to *colour 2*.
Row 3: Knit all stitches.
Row 4: Purl all stitches.
Change to *colour 1*.
Now you simply repeat rows 1 – 4 (including the colour changes) five more times (24 rows in total).
Row 25: (using *colour 1*) Knit all stitches.
Row 26: Purl all stitches.
Cast off.

Making up

Sew in any loose ends. Stitch the long edges of the candy cane together and then the bottom of the candy cane using mattress stitch, leaving a gap at the top. Cut the pipe cleaner to twice as long as your knitting and fold the pipe cleaner in half. Insert the pipe cleaner into the knitted tube, then seal the top by stitching. Bend the candy cane into shape, now stitch the brooch back to the seam you have created! ❑

WINTER WONDERLAND

I ♥ Snow Scarf

This winter warmer is highly patterned and makes a thick and cosy scarf. Knitted in the round, the patterning is worked using knit stitch only, and stranded yarns are kept hidden away inside the knitted tube!

Before you start...

Difficulty Rating:

- Finished size approx 18cm by 165cm.
- Tension, 23 stitches and 20 rows to 10cm over patterned stocking stitch using 4mm needles.
- See video 2 for stocking stitch and video 11 for stranded knitting instructions.

You will need...

- ✓ 4mm circular needle, 40cm long.
- ✓ Three balls King Cole Merino Blend DK wool in Black (*colour 1*).
- ✓ Two balls King Cole Merino Blend DK wool in Scarlet (*colour 2*).
- ✓ Three balls King Cole Merino Blend DK wool in Snow White (*colour 3*).
- ✓ Tapestry Needle

Knitting the Scarf

This scarf is knitted in stocking stitch in the round, with a purl stitch at the start of each pattern row; this purl stitch is included to define the divide between the front and back of the scarf and make a natural fold. When working from the chart, strand yarn across back, taking care to not pull too tight as this would distort the pattern and not let the scarf lie flat.

Using *colour 1*, cast on 86 stitches.

Begin knitting in rounds as follows:Round 1: Purl 1 st, knit 42 sts, purl 1 st, knit 42 sts.

Continue working in stocking stitch and purl stitches as round 1, and follow chart from round 2, working the chart twice for each round. ▷

Chart

■ *Colour 1*
■ *Colour 2*
  Colour 3
  Purl Stitch

I heart Snow Chart
Work 7 repeats of the chart.
Cast off.

Making up
You will now have a beautiful
knitted tube, to turn this into
a wearable scarf just neatly
overstitch the ends together,
closing the open edges. ❑

WHAT A
SWEETIE!

Hot-water bottle Cover

This project is great for beginners. Worked in stocking stitch stripe, the knitting is easy and the simple finishing touches turn it into a super sweet hot-water bottle cover!

Before you start...

Difficulty Rating:

- Finished size when made up approx 21cm by 50cm
- Tension, 20 stitches and 30 rows to 10cm over stocking stitch using 4mm needles.
- See video 1 for garter stitch and video 2 for stocking stitch instructions.

You will need...

✓ Pair 4mm knitting needles.
✓ Two balls King Cole Merino Blend DK wool in Dusky Pink (colour 1).
✓ One ball King Cole Merino Blend DK wool in Scarlet (colour 2).
✓ Tapestry needle.
✓ 80cms of 30mm-wide red ribbon.
✓ Sewing needle and red thread.

Knitting

Using *colour 1*, cast on 80 stitches.
Knit 4 rows in garter stitch (knitting all stitches).
Row 5: Purl all stitches.
Row 6: Knit all stitches.
Rows 7 – 36: Continue working stocking stitch by repeating rows 5 and 6.
Rows 37 – 44: Change to *colour 2*, work 8 rows stocking stitch.
Rows 45 – 52: Change to *colour 1*, work 8 rows stocking stitch.

The stripes continue through the body of this hot water bottle cover, repeat rows 37 – 52 three more times.

Rows 101 – 108: Change to *colour 2*, work 8 rows stocking stitch.
Now changing back to *colour 1* for the end.
Rows 109 – 142: Work in stocking stitch.
Now knit 4 rows garter stitch (knitting all stitches).
Cast off. ▷

Making Up
Sew in all loose yarn ends. Block the piece well. Fold it in half widthways with the back of the knitting facing you. Sew up the long side of this piece, turn right way out.

Now to add the ribbon, you will be securing one of the ends and leaving the other open. Cut your ribbon into two 40cm pieces, line up the centre of the ribbon with the back centre of the knitted hot water bottle cover. Stitch the ribbon to the back of the case (see diagram, below).

Now tie one of the ribbons in a bow, and secure this bow by stitching through the centre creating the one closed end. The other end remains open; you can secure it by tying the ribbon around the water bottle neck. ❑

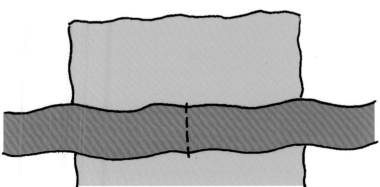

▲ Stitching the bow

INSTRUCTIONALS

Kandy's Code-Breaker

Below is a full list of explanations of all the abbreviations that I have used throughout this book.

k	=	Knit.
k1	=	Knit one stitch.
p	=	Purl.
p1	=	Purl one stitch.
st	=	Stitch.
sl1	=	Slip one stitch.
sts	=	Stitches.
inc	=	Increase.
pw	=	Purl wise, as if to purl.
psso	=	Pass the slip stitch over.
k2tog	=	Knit two stitches together.
p2tog	=	Purl two stitches together.

 Knit and Destroy... Gets Handy!

sl 1
Slip one stitch, simply slip a stitch from the left needle onto the right needle without knitting it.

psso
Passing a slipped stitch over a knitted stitch, the stitch is passed over in the same way as the loop is when casting off.

garter stitch
Knitting every stitch on every row.

stocking stitch
Knit all stitches on one row, purl all stitches on next row, repeat.

Picking up stitches
Insert empty needle into relevant stitches, then on first row work (knit/purl according to pattern) across the picked up stitches.

stranding colours
This is used when working with more than one colour of yarn. The yarn not in use is carried loosely (if you pull it tight this will distort the pattern) across the back of your knitting.

following a chart
When following a pattern chart, always start at the bottom and work your way up. For stocking stitch, you will work across the first line from right to left, then across the following line from left to right.

blocking
This is the method used to make sure your knitting lies flat ready to sew up, or just to wear! Simply pin your knit out on your ironing board, you can check it's the right size at this stage, stretch it slightly if needed. You will then press the piece of knitting to smooth it out and help it hold shape. To do this, lay a damp cloth on top of your knitting and steam the piece thoroughly then press with your iron, lightly and evenly (through the cloth) lifting the iron to make sure you're not dragging your knitting.

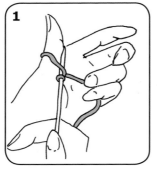

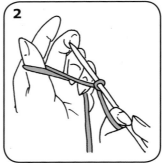

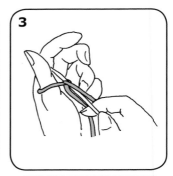

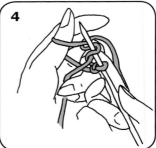

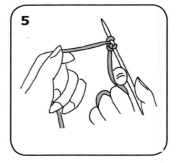

Cast On ▶

This is my preferred cast on method as you only use one needle. You will need to judge where to make the initial slip knot. A slip knot 30cm from the end will give you enough yarn to cast on about 20 stitches.

1: To start, make a slip knot at the required distance from the end of the yarn. Put the slip knot onto the needle and place the needle in your right hand. *Now wind the loose end of yarn (not attached to the ball) clockwise around your left thumb.

2: Slide the needle under the loop of yarn around your thumb.

3: With your right forefinger, take the ball yarn between the needle and your thumb then over the point of the needle.

4: Take the knitting needle with the loop around it through the yarn loop on your left thumb

5: Take your thumb out of the loop and pull the loose end to secure the stitch*.

Repeat from * until you have the required number of stitches on the needle.

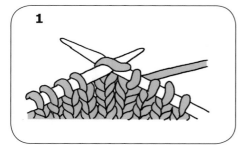

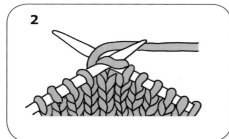

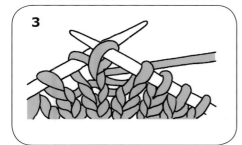

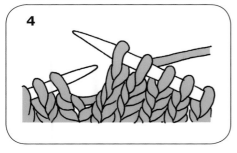

◄ K – Knit Stitch

1: IN – with the yarn at the back of your knitting, insert the tip of the right hand needle (from left to right) through the next stitch on the left hand needle

2: OVER – wind the yarn from behind around the tip of the right hand needle

3: THROUGH – pull the point of the right needle and the new yarn loop on it through the stitch

4: OFF – slip the original stitch off the left hand needle.

Repeat these steps until all the stitches have moved from the left to the right needle.

P – Purl stitch ▶

1: UP – with the yarn at the front of your knitting, insert the point of the needle from right to left, up through the first stitch

2: OVER – wind the yarn over the tip of the right-hand needle

3: THROUGH – pull the point of the right-hand needle and the new yarn loop through the stitch

4: OFF – slip the original stitch off the left-hand needle.

Repeat these steps until all the stitches have moved from the left to the right needle.

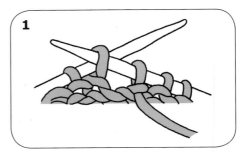

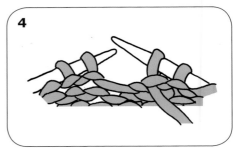

▲ Inc1
(Increase on a Knit Row)

Working into the front and back of a stitch. Knit into the stitch as normal, but, before slipping it off the needle knit again, this time into the back of the stitch then slip it off the needle.

▲ Inc1 pw
(Increase on a Purl Row)

Working into the front and back of a stitch. Purl into the stitch as normal, but, before slipping it off the needle, purl again, this time into the back of the stitch then slip it off the needle.

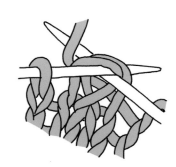

▲ k2tog
Knit Two Together

This is a decrease and it is done by simply working two stitches together.
Insert the right hand needle (from left to right) through the next two stitches on the left hand needle, then knit them together like they are one stitch.

Purl Two Together

Insert the right hand needle (from right to left) through the next two stitches on the left hand needle, then knit them together like they are one stitch.

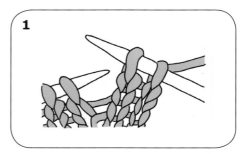

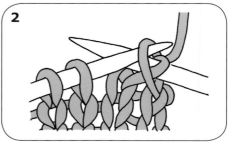

Cast Off ▶

Always cast off using the stitch that you have been knitting with. For example, when casting off stocking stitch you cast off using the knit stitch on a knit row and using purl if casting off on a purl row. Casting off a rib should be done as if you were continuing to rib the pattern.

1. Knit (or purl) the first two stitches
2. *Insert the tip of the left hand needle into the first stitch you knitted and lift it over the second second stitch.
3. Drop this stitch off both needles.
4. Knit the next stitch then repeat from* until you have cast off all the stitches. When you have only one stitch left on the right hand needle cut the yarn 15cm from the knitting.

Now slip the stitch off the needle and feed the end through the last loop, pull tight to secure.

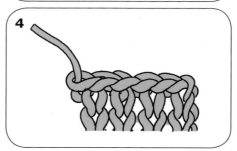

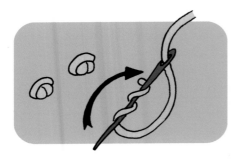

French knot ▲

This little neat knot is great for small circular details. To start, bring the needle up through the fabric then wind the yarn twice around the needle. Now simply take the needle back through the fabric at the same point pulling the yarn through, creating a small knot on the surface of the fabric.

Backstitch ▼

This hand-stitch is great for decoration because it creates a continuous line. To start, bring the needle up through the fabric and make the first stitch by pushing the needle into the fabric a short distance behind where you just brought the needle through the fabric. Now bring the needle back through to the front of the fabric in front of the thread by the same distance. Repeat this motion, always bringing the needle back to the previous stitch.

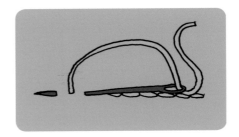

Mattress Stitch ▶

This stitch is a magic way to create an invisible seam on your knitting. It works because you sew between the vertical rows on the knitting and the stitches are covered.

With your tapestry needle threaded with a long piece of yarn knotted at the end, place the two seams side by side in front of you. Secure the yarn to the corner of the right hand side piece of fabric by bringing the needle through from the back to front of the fabric.

Now, working into the left hand piece first, take the needle through the fabric between the first two stitches on the first row and push the needle up under the bars of two stitches and pull the yarn through. Now, in the same way, take the needle under two bars on the right hand piece of fabric. **(See diagram 1)**

Keep repeating this all the way along your seam, switching sides after each stitch, making sure that the needle has been taken under each bar on each side to make a secure seam. **(See diagram 2)**

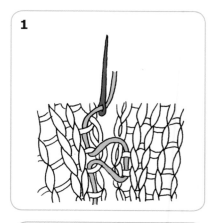

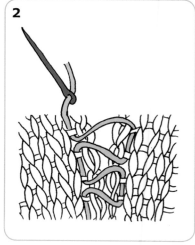

Acknowledgements

This book may have my name on it... but its success has relied on lots of other people helping out in all kinds of ways, giving up their time and resources to help make this project a reality!

Firstly, I'd like to thank the knitters; Rachel, Josephine and Kathryn (aka Mum) who helped to turn the patterns featured into physical knitted items. Extra thanks go to my mum for her patience and support, and for sharing her knitting expertise!

Thanks to Maria for her magic with the camera, making the knits look fantastic, and the amazing models, Alison and Lee, who were naturals in front of the lens, and extremely patient with mine and Maria's direction – and our constant cheap laughs!

A massive thank you to Ben for his illustration skills; the ability to turn my few words of instruction into the exact thing I was imagining, and for his constant help, support, tea and flapjacks.

Thanks to Seleena for making *Sugar Paper* zine with me for all these years and for the powerful D.I.Y attitude, without which I would never have been able to do this.

Thanks to Suzy and Ian of Cabin Creative, for taking on this project in the first place, and for working so hard to turn my ideas into a real life book. And a special thanks to King Cole Yarns, who generously supplied all the yarn needed for testing and knitting all the patterns you see in this book free of charge!

Kandy